The Trial of Eddie Gallagher, Navy SEAL

By
Acie Cargill

Synopsis

This was a very newsworthy case of a Navy SEAL accused of murdering an ISIS prisoner of war by stabbing him in the neck after trying to save his life with emergency medical procedures. Everything about the case was controversial including that Gallagher was accused by other SEALS under his command who resented the extreme combat situations Gallagher subjected them to. Gallagher himself was a highly decorated war hero from fighting in Iraq and Afghanistan and he felt the new S EAL recruits were soft and even cowardly. It was the old school against the new.

Eventually Gallagher was found not guilty for the killing of the prisoner and his record was mostly exonerated except that he posed with the body of the dead ISIS fighter. It was a far lesser charge and instead of life in prison, Gallagher just took a cut in his rank and pay. President Trump got involved and hinted that he would pardon Gallagher if he was found guilty, and the President sent him a congratulatory note when he was found innocent.

About the Author

 Acie Cargill is a poet, a songwriter, and a prose writer. He studied poetry with USA Poet Laureate Mark Strand and Illinois Poet Laureate Gwendolyn Brooks. He studied novel writing with Thomas Berger, who wrote Little Big Man (that Arthur Penn made into a movie with Dustin Hoffman in the lead role). Cargill also studied journalism with instructor Jean Daily. His work is a synthesis of all these styles.

He is a member of American Mensa and formerly Edited the Mensa Journal of Poetry. He also is a member of the Grammy Association, and The US Quill and Scroll Society.

Cargill is a vegetarian, a former holistic physician, a musical performer on a variety of instruments, an environmental activist, a lecturer, medical reviewer, a lover, and a seer.

Website

http://aciecargill.com

Contact

aciecargill@gmail.com

Other Books Written by the Author:

Puerto Rico

Aberrations

Chronicles

Terrorism

Modern Love

Ends and odds

Illiana: The Border Area Between Illinois and Indiana

Pullman

Che and Fidel - A Reading Play of the Cuban Revolution

Celia Sanchez - A Play of the Cuban Revolution

Paschke - A Play

Gwendolyn Brooks: A Play

Rasputin - A Play

Nietzsche - A Play

Bob Dylan, The Early Years - A Musical Play

Michael Jackson - A Play

Einstein - A Biographical Play

El Chapo - A Play In 3 Acts

Raisins and Roaches - A Three Month Diary of a Crack Addict

Susan B. Anthony - A Biographical Play

Kankakee

Harriet Tubman - A Biographical Play

Tesla - A Biographical Play

Vegan Saint - A Play in 3 Acts

Martin Luther King, Jr - A Play

Great Migration: A Play in 3 Acts

George Pullman - A Play in Three Acts

Frederick Douglass - A Biographical Play

Freud - A Biographical Play in 3 Acts

The Underground Railroad - An Educational Play

Payton, Jordan, Ali - A Biographical Play

Mr. Nobody - A Play

The Kid From Left Field - A Play

Puerto Rico, A Dream of Independence - A Play in 3 Acts

Crack Madness - A Monologue Play

Johnny Appleseed - A Family Play

Dr. Jekll and Mr. Hyde - A Modernized Play

Obama - Obama - A Play In 3 Acts

Will Rogers - A Biographical Monologue

Merle Haggard - A Biographical Monologue

Mother Teresa - A Biographical Monologue

Gwendolyn Brooks - A Biographical Monologue

Love Life of Susan B. Anthony - A Monologue Play

Sojourner Truth - A Biographical Monologue plus Narrator

Harriet Tubman and The Underground Railroad - A Play

Helen Keller, Words and Wisdom - A Biographical Play

Eugene Debs and the 1894 Pullman Strike - A Play

The Rising - A Play

Walt Disney - A Biographical One Act Play

The Experiments of Dr. Victor Frankenstein - A Play - Based on the novel by Mary Shelley

Karl Marx - A One Act Play

Martin Luther at The Diet of Worms - A One Act Play

Martin Luther King: Monologue and Narrator Play

Frederick Douglass - Monologue and Narrator Play

Kaepernick - A One Act Play

Settling South Holland - A Play In 2 Acts

Kaepernick - A Full-Length Play

My Son Died From An Overdose - A Play

Overdose - A One Act Play

Always a Marine First

Erotic Muslim Polygamy

George Dolton's Bridge to Freedom Underground Railroad - A One-Act Play

Greta Thunberg - A One-Act Play About Climate Change

A Brief History of the Philippines

Goat With No Horns - Voodoo Cannibals in Haiti

Johnny Cash - Monologue Play

Muhammad Words Of Wisdom

Jesus Words Of Wisdom

Bob Hope - Biographical Monologue

The Cargills of Graves County, Ky

Keith Raniere and the NXIVM Sex Club

Words of Wisdom – Native Americans, Ancient Greeks, Buddha and African-Americans

Words of Wisdom – Mark Twain, Benjamin Franklin, Shakespeare and Solomon

Table of Contents

1. Introduction

If you are faint-hearted in a war, you will probably lose whatever you are fighting for and maybe your life. Navy SEALs are the elite fighters in the United States armed forces. They have to do all the dirty work. The hardest jobs. Most dangerous. They must be fearless with no qualms about killing the enemy. Killing is about equal to eating. Just something that must be done to survive.

The war with ISIS is an especially dirty war. Always someone waiting to kill you. Most people cannot begin to understand what these American fighters are experiencing. Hardly anyone appreciates their efforts and hardly anyone even knows what they do. It is not fighting with soldiers who are governed by any moral restraints. Not because they are Muslim, but because they are ruthless killers. Behead their captives. Brutality towards women. Torture. Just about every heinous quality imaginable. All for some sort of perverted religious beliefs. Those are the worst. When the cruelty is done in the name of a religion. No holds barred then.

Eddie Gallagher is a master fighter for the American SEALs. He is one of the most decorated heroes. He wasn't awarded the Medal of Honor. Those are pretty rare and usually posthumous, but he won about every other honor possible. One act of bravery after another. The man was made of courage. 19 years in the military fighting for what he believed in. Following orders. Always placing duty above his own safety. Now he is on trial by an American military tribunal

1

attempting to have him spend the rest of his life behind bars..
Accused of losing his restraints and exacting personal
vengeance against the hated ISIS enemy. Maybe he did. And
maybe with good reason.

Maybe with no reason. Maybe he just lost it after 19 years of
extreme warfare. Doesn't that seem possible? If so, should he
be incarcerated in a military prison for life? The man is one of
America's greatest heroes. Maybe he needs help. Isn't that
understandable. He just took what he believed to be his duty
to an extreme. Maybe he is insane. After 19 years of life and
death pressures, isn't that understandable.

2. Death of Ahmed

None of the Americans really know the ISIS teenager's name. ISIS keeps those things very private. When you fight for ISIS you are nameless. Even your parents are told to forget you because your body and soul now belong to Allah. For purposes of this story, he will be named Ahmed. It is estimated he was 15 years old, a handsome, beardless black-¬haired youth who had been hiding and fighting in a safehouse that was hit by an American missile. He was captured by Iraqi ground troops and taken to the American Seals for possible medical help.

Often when people are hit by missiles their lungs are blasted and almost beyond repair. He was gasping for air and struggled out of the house and was shot several times by the Iraqi troops, but he was still alive. Just barely. Suffering terribly. Unable to breathe. This was a battle zone not a modern hospital. No lung transplants available. Ahmed was dying and could probably not be saved with any available procedures. He was fighting for Allah and would soon join him in his paradise.

The Navy SEALS are trained in rudimentary life saving techniques, Some are medics, but most learn to do what they can to save their fellow SEALS when they are wounded in battle. A SEAL inserted a chest tube into Ahmed and Eddie Gallagher used a special kit and performed a cricothyroidotomy — or "cric" — a simple and rapid surgical method for opening up a blocked airway by inserting a tube through an incision in the cricothyroid ligament. Other SEALS inserted a trachea tube, two chest tubes and a Sternal Intraosseous Infusion, which bores through the sternum bone to reach veins when other IVs won't work. These guys were really trying to save this ISIS fighter.

At the time that the ISIS fighter was brought to the SEAL compound, he was at or near death and, although Gallagher initially attempted to save his life, these efforts quickly proved to be fruitless. Once it was clear that the ISIS fighter was beyond saving, the platoon's medic ... took over and began using the newly dead or nearly dead ISIS fighter as a training aid to practice performing medical procedures. Other Seals had been recording the procedures with their helmet cameras, but they turned them off.

The actual cause of death of Ahmed has been in debate. The body was taken away by the Iraqi's and was never available again to be examined. The platoon medic admitted to using the dying ISIS fighter's body for invasive and unnecessary procedures for his skills development and to demonstrate to the other SEALS present. One of the them claims he saw Gallagher stab the prisoner in

the throat with a knife, but he did not mention any blood flow which should have occurred if Ahmed was still alive at the time. Gallagher directed the attempt to save Ahmed's life but it was unsuccessful.

3. From Sean Gallagher, Eddie's brother

Sean Gallagher is the brother of Eddie Gallagher. They are part of an extensive military family that includes their father, a West Point graduate and retired Lieutenant Colonel, two uncles who were naval aviators and three grandparents who served in the Navy during World War II.

It's been said a lie can travel halfway around the world before the truth has a chance to put on its shoes. Or, to use a more modern rendition of the phrase, fake news catches fire before the truth can be used to put it out. These phrases may seem impersonal, but what happens if the lie is about your loved ones? What happens if the liars have the backing of the federal government and the fake news they're spewing threatens to take down an American hero?

This is what's happening to my family right now, as the most untrue of allegations have been made, and the most sinister of tactics have been used to spread them.

My brother is Eddie Gallagher, a father of three and decorated U.S. Navy SEAL, now confined behind razor wire in military jail. He's served this country for nearly two decades and has always been the humble hero of our family. His accolades, even among the elite warriors he serves with, stand out: multiple awards for valor, good conduct, bravery, leadership—all given at an increasing pace over his experienced career. This upcoming spring, after twenty long years and eight combat tours, he was looking forward to hanging up his uniform and spending time with his family. If anyone has earned it, Eddie has.

But earlier this year—due to a mixture of ego, incompetence, and careerism, —what started out as the grumblings of a few disgruntled subordinates has turned into insane allegations of war crimes. Our family is now fighting the battle of our lives, pushing back against an onslaught of falsehoods and a pack of government lawyers hell-bent on "taking down" a Navy SEAL.

On his last deployment to Mosul, President Trump tasked Eddie and his platoon to clear ISIS from the Iraqi city, and they succeeded in that mission. There was intense combat, and as the leader, Eddie pushed his men hard. There were grinding days of continual firefights, clearing hostile territory, and dealing with one of the cruelest enemies in human history.

Eddie said some younger sailors in his platoon were weaker than others, began to break, and complained of being pushed too hard. They were new to the SEAL teams, had never seen combat, and didn't know the reality of the war they were tasked with fighting. They said Eddie took them on too many missions, exposed them to too much danger, risked their lives too easily.

So a small mutiny began.

Eddie reacted swiftly. He gathered the small crew of complainers, publicly reprimanded them, and benched them to the back lines. This was, after all, an elite fighting force, where men train relentlessly for years for the opportunity like this to fight terrorists. After being sequestered, Eddie allowed these junior sailors to rejoin the platoon, thinking they'd learned their lesson and start performing.

However, after being let back in, they never got over being rebuked. Being called cowards in combat is a career killer. You have to understand that in the SEAL teams, reputation is everything—you can imagine how important having confidence in the man next to you is during a firefight. These younger guys expected a bad review, knew their careers were at stake, and thus began to tell stories about Eddie's leadership and actions in combat. They figured if he were under investigation before he retired he couldn't stall or impact their careers.

And so just like that, a hellish process began to take shape. What started as trying to make complaints in-house to discredit Eddie turned into something much bigger than they expected. Investigators were involved now, and the process began snowball out of control.

Ed was notified he was under investigation months after returning home but naively assumed his command and investigators would see through the absurdity of what was being said. After all, the claims of this small group defied eyewitnesses, defied logic, and were downright outrageous.

Previously lauded for his level-headedness and steady leadership, they say Eddie suddenly, without reason, "became unhinged." Even though it would have been impossible for someone not to see, he went on shooting sprees. A superior marksman, Eddie suddenly couldn't tell that his rifle had been purposely tampered with by his own team-mates. Then, after performing life-saving maneuvers on a wounded ISIS fighter, Eddie, for no reason, killed him.

These accusations would be laughable—and were to him and our family—until for some crazy reason the Navy took them seriously.

Multiple—and I quite literally mean multiple—of Eddie's teammates on his last deployment deny all of what has been said about him. My brother will have a team of witnesses come to his side to refute all of these false charges. Even the Iraqi General serving with Eddie's platoon denies that the alleged events took place.

However, if you read the news or dare to venture into the cesspool of social media, my brother is apparently a lunatic. It's already over, according to the keyboard crusaders. In the court of public opinion, under the deluge clickbait articles taken straight from the government's mouth, the case is closed.

The most infuriating part of this whole charade for our family has been the actions of the Navy, in particular NCIS and Navy prosecutors.

From the beginning, it's been a coordinated smear campaign so they could make themselves look good by painting him as a monster. He takes prescribed pain medication for a damaged disc in his back, so they threw in a drug charge. He vented to friends about how this whole investigation is a farce; suddenly he's obstructing justice. Prosecutors actually had the gall to use a text message argument between him and his wife about leaving a movie theatre early to insinuate spousal abuse. These are the steps the prosecution is taking to grasp at anything—literally anything—to smear the name of a good man.

This tactic, of painting Eddie as a villain, is a playbook used by prosecutors time and again to distance themselves from responsibility, muddy the waters, and convince you emotionally that he must be guilty.

During the closing arguments of Eddie's probable cause hearing, the Navy prosecutor empathized with ISIS, saying Eddie is the reason they kill. He actually said those words, out loud, about a man who joined the service out of high school, has fought in every conflict since 9/11, has risked life and limb, and signed right back up to do it again and again for his country. Imagine for a second someone said brave WWII soldiers were the reason Hitler became a tyrant. The insanity of such statements should make your blood boil, and yet, Navy prosecutors are using your tax dollars to call a war hero a PR tool for ISIS.

If Eddie had died on this last deployment, which was something that almost happened, there would have been parades. His wife, two sons, daughter and I would have attended ceremonies and speeches, even from his accusers, about his bravery. But he survived and has come home to find himself the target of the very country he's fought to protect for decades.

In the brig, my brother, a man of incredible resolve, actually uttered the words, "It may have been better if they killed me over there. At least I knew who the enemy was."

It's been said a lie can travel around the world before the truth can put its shoes on. Well, our family has our shoes on now and we're suiting up for battle. From our viewpoint, Eddie has fought for us for twenty years. It's now our honor to fight for him. Join us.

4. Eddie Gallagher's Military Career

Eddie Gallagher enlisted in the US military in 1999 and served for 19 years with eight overseas deployments, including service in both the Iraq War and the War in Afghanistan. He was trained as a medic, a sniper, and as an explosives expert. During his service, he was decorated for valor several times, including two Bronze Stars. He has received positive evaluations from his superiors within the SEALs and served as an instructor in the SEALs BUD/S program for recruits. Gallagher goes by the nickname "Blade" with his fellow frogmen.

Gallagher also attracted controversies and investigations, although few formal reprimands. He was the subject in an investigation of the shooting of a young girl in Afghanistan in 2010, but was cleared of wrongdoing in it. He also allegedly tried to run over a Navy police officer with his car in 2014 after being detained at a traffic stop. By 2015, Gallagher had acquired a reputation as someone who was more interested in fighting terrorists and less interested in compliance with rules. In his eighth deployment in 2017, Gallagher's aggressive side was seemingly amplified, especially during the Battle for Mosul, wherein the US force mission was intended to be more advisory than direct combat. Gallagher was the subject of a number of reports from his fellow SEAL team members of actions not in keeping with the rules of war, but initially these reports were dismissed by the SEAL command structure. Only after the reports were escalated outside the

SEALs were they acted upon and directed to the Naval Criminal Investigative Service (NCIS). On September 11, 2018, Gallagher was arrested at Camp Pendleton and charged with premeditated murder, attempted murder, obstruction of justice, and other offenses. On October 18, Lieutenant Jacob Portier of Gallagher's platoon was also charged with failing to properly escalate to his superiors in the chain of command as well as destroying evidence. Gallagher pleaded not guilty to all the charges against him.

5. Why this Case Happened

The SEALs who went after Gallagher had a number of motives for bringing the chief down, including derailing his advancement to senior chief and a proposed Silver Star medal for combat valor.

Others seemed to want to get him fired from a training position Gallagher held, according to legal filings.

"They wanted Gallagher removed," his lawyer Tim Parlatore said on Saturday. "Reputations are everything on the SEAL Teams, and they were worried about what he would tell people about their performance in Iraq.

"He was calling them 'cowards' in country, mostly just to motivate them to get off their asses and fight, and they resented that and worried he'd do that in California — that what happened on deployment wouldn't stay on deployment.

"They didn't understand that he wasn't going to do that."

Parlatore suspects that after NCIS started interviewing them they began to realize that they were stuck with stories they had to repeat, or face charges for lying to investigators.

And then on Jan. 22, military prosecutors indicted Alpha Platoon's officer in charge, Lt. Jacob "Jake" Portier, for allegedly helping to cover up Gallagher's misconduct, accusations the Navy officer also strongly denies.

"Jake is collateral damage and they didn't want to become collateral damage themselves," Parlatore said.

A former Surface Warfare Officer, Parlatore plans to personally cross-examine Naval Special Warfare Operator 1st Class medic Terrance "TC" Byrne; SEAL snipers SO1 Dalton Tolbert, SO2 Joshua Vriens, and SO1 Dylan Dille — now a civilian — plus one of their junior officers, Lt. Tom MacNeil.

The Navy and U.S. Department of Justice provided them immunity deals against prosecution in exchange for their testimony against Gallagher and Portier.

"This is a case that never should've been brought in the first place," Parlatore said. "The prosecution and NCIS utterly failed in their duties to properly investigate this case and find the truth. Because of their failures, an innocent man is going on trial.

"But we're confident that the jury will see the truth and Eddie Gallagher will be found not guilty. The days of these witnesses hiding in the shadows to try to destroy their chief's life with their lies are over and they now have to answer for their false statements.".

Only Miller and Byrne allegedly witnessed portions of Gallagher's interaction with the prisoner. The rest are expected to testify about the alleged shootings and accusations that Gallagher sought to cover up the crimes.

It appears that the new prosecution team will lean heavily on photos taken shortly after the prisoner's death.

One shows Gallagher holding the teen's hair and brandishing a knife and the other depicts the chief re-enlisting near his remains.

They'll also bring up a text message Gallagher sent that seems to suggest he slayed someone with a knife, talk Parlatore has written off as the sort of "dark humor" shared between combat veterans.

Gallagher made no effort to hide the knife or its sheaf. Trace analysis of the blade turned up only a skin cell, not blood, that could belong to a Middle Eastern man, according to court filings.

No DNA was found in the leather carrier, where any blood should've dripped, Parlatore added.

No bodies of any alleged victims were unearthed so no autopsies were performed.

Digital videos of the Islamic State fighter were recorded before he died, but the helmet camera was turned off at a key moment in the footage and someone deleted multiple files that should've contained other images.

In their legal filings, prosecutors have only said that they can't locate the missing files and haven't suggested a motive for why they were destroyed.

Gallagher's legal team believes the footage likely exonerated him, which is why the evidence disappeared.

Parlatore expects a Marine Raider, Staff Sgt. Giorgio Kirylo, and two Iraqi leaders — Iraqi Emergency Response Division commander Maj. Gen. Abbas al-Jubouri and his aide, Col. Issa Kadhim — will testify that Gallagher didn't kill the prisoner.

But the most important testimony might come from Scott, who had been monitoring the detainee before he died..

Investigative records, a letter to Navy officials and messages provided to Navy Times show that Scott told investigators that the Islamic State prisoner was nearly dead when brought into the compound and that his fellow SEALs began a series of procedures on the teenager that weren't medically necessary.

That matched other documents provided to Navy Times that showed a number of medical procedures performed on the prisoner over the span of about 20 minutes.

They included a cricothyroidotomy — or "cric" — a simple and rapid surgical method for opening up a blocked airway by inserting a tube through an incision in the cricothyroid ligament, plus a trachea tube, at least two chest tubes and a Sternal Intraosseous Infusion, which bores through bone to reach veins when other IVs won't work, records indicate.

That all could be medically necessary to save a man from death, but defense attorneys will paint a more macabre picture of the prisoner's last moments and suggest that the detainee died long before Gallagher allegedly stabbed him.

"Once it was clear that the ISIS fighter was beyond saving, the platoon's medic, SO1 T.C. Byrne, took over and began using the newly dead or nearly dead ISIS fighter as a training aid to practice performing medical procedures," defense attorneys wrote in a May 26 motion to Rugh.

16

"The possibility that SO1 Byrne and other members of the team were performing, for skill development, medically nonindicated invasive medical procedures on a newly dead or dying ISIS fighter is significant for a number of reasons and should have been immediately disclosed to the defense," they added.

In their motion, defense attorneys alleged that several witnesses for the prosecution gave statements that were either inaccurately depicted by Warpinski in his reports "or inaccurately given out of fear that the truth would lead to charges against either SO1 Byrne or the witnesses themselves."

But in his interview with NCIS and in motions filed by prosecutors, Byrne offered a different take.

He told investigators that the detainee arrived in the compound with a leg injury — the Iraqis said he'd been shot trying to escape a safe house after an airstrike destroyed it — and labored to breathe, possibly from "blast lung," a condition that often afflicts patients who survive explosions.

Byrne "left the scene, and when he returned, he was surprised to find the prisoner dead," prosecutors wrote.

If he repeats that in his sworn testimony, it will be Byrne and Miller against Scott, Kirylo, the Iraqi officers and possibly others.

How a jury of commissioned officers and senior chief and master chief petty officers weigh the credibility of their testimony could determine Gallagher's fate

6. The Trial

Gallagher's defense team rested its case Friday, two days after it began calling witnesses to refute the narrative put forth by Navy prosecutors who said Gallagher not only killed the young prisoner, but also posed for photos next to his corpse, shot at noncombatants and intimidated other SEALs who might report him. The actions allegedly occurred during his deployment to Mosul, Iraq, in 2017.

Gallagher, a special operations chief, pleaded not guilty to the charges in January. If convicted of murder, he faces life in prison.

The case has caught the eye of President Donald Trump, who has expressed sympathy for Gallagher on Twitter and is reportedly mulling a pardon for the SEAL.

Here's a breakdown of the cases Navy prosecutors and Gallagher's defense attorneys have presented over nearly the past two weeks, based on witness testimony.

The prosecution rested its case after calling 14 witnesses in six days, including fellow SEALs who served alongside Gallagher and testified their chief stabbed a young ISIS prisoner and shot at noncombatants, including elderly men and young teenage girls.

The stakes are highest for Gallagher when it comes to the accusation that he stabbed a teenage ISIS prisoner, whom one witness described as frail, weak and injured.

Witnesses say Navy SEAL took photos with a corpse and shot at unarmed civilians

Other SEALs who served alongside Gallagher testified they saw Gallagher stab the ISIS fighter. SEAL Special Operations Chief Craig Miller testified he saw Gallagher stab the prisoner "on the right side of his neck, toward the jugular vein."

A forensic pathologist later testified that the stabbing described by the witnesses "could result in massive hemorrhaging into the chest ... or death."

He conceded on cross-examination he could not determine the actual cause of death -- there was no known autopsy -- and made his conclusion based on the information and evidence he was provided, including photos and witness testimony.

Several SEALs testified during the first week they saw Gallagher take pictures with the body. Miller and Officer Thomas MacNeil both admitted to taking a group photo with the body. MacNeil said he didn't know the circumstances of the prisoner's death at the time.

Miller realized that was unprofessional, he said, adding he immediately reported the killing to his superior. He testified that Gallagher later asked him, "Who's not good with it?"

Former SEAL Dylan Dille told the court he saw Gallagher pose for individual and group photos with the body. Dille never posed for the photos because he said he "felt it was irresponsible."

Following the alleged stabbing, MacNeil said he and others were told to delete the photos. He claimed Gallagher later said, "If you take me down, I'll take all of you down."

According to Dille, upon returning to base, Gallagher told him and other SEALs, "I know you're not alright with what happened, but it's just an ISIS dirtbag. Next time if I get a prisoner, I'll do this where you can't see what happens."

Dille also said that during a sniper mission he saw Gallagher shoot at civilians, including an elderly man and two women in hijabs. In the case of the elderly man, Dille said they were in position and saw two men standing on a corner. He heard a rifle shot; one man was hit, struggled, but got away.

Dille testified he heard Gallagher say over the radio, "Oh I thought I missed."

Dalton Tolbert, another witness, said he fired a warning shot at an old man during a sniper mission with Gallagher. The man ran away, Tolbert said, but fell after another sniper fired. Tolbert claimed he heard a voice that sounded like Gallagher on the radio say, "You guys missed but I got him."

A third witness said he heard shots fired from Gallagher's position during another sniper mission. Joshua Vriens said he saw four girls who looked to be between the ages of 12 and

14. After the shot, one girl clutched her stomach and fell down.

All three admitted on cross-examination they did not actually see Gallagher fire the shot. Dille said he based his accusation on the vapor trail that he said emanated from Gallagher's position.

Witness testimony adds major twist to Navy SEAL's trial

On cross-examination, Tolbert was confronted by defense attorneys about texts he sent in a group chat with other SEALs shortly before the trial started. Two of them said, "Somebody fire this p***y a** f*****g judge" and "This legal process is a joke."

Tolert said the messages were written out of frustration.

The defense's case

Defense attorney Tim Parlatore has portrayed Gallagher as an "old-school, hard-charging warrior," targeted by his younger comrades who harbored a "personal animosity" toward him.

Perhaps the most compelling moment of the defense team's case came during its cross-examination of one of the prosecution's own witnesses.

Special Operator First Class Corey Scott, a SEAL medic, said that while he'd seen Gallagher stab the prisoner, he was the one who "suffocated" him.

"I held my thumb over his trach tube until he asphyxiated," he said, referring to a tube inserted into the prisoner's neck during a tracheotomy to help him breathe.

He suggested it was an act of mercy because he was concerned the boy -- a prisoner of the Iraqi forces -- would be tortured by the Iraqis.

Scott, who testified under immunity, had not admitted to killing the prisoner in previous interviews with investigators and prosecutors.

The defense made a motion to dismiss the case based on Scott's testimony, but was denied.

According to an email obtained by CNN earlier this week, Navy prosecutors are exploring a possible perjury charge against Scott. The email from the Navy to Scott's lawyer said he "reportedly testified directly contrary to previous official statements -- thus exposing him to prosecution."

Navy officials at the Pentagon declined to comment on the potential charges, as did Scott's attorney.

There were tense exchanges between defense attorneys and investigators from the Naval Criminal Investigative Service (NCIS) who raided Gallagher's home and looked for evidence.

On cross-examination, Parlatore aggressively questioned investigator Brian Frank, who led the raid on the home. The defense attorney claimed two of Gallagher's children -- who were 8 and 18 at the time -- "were dragged out of their house in their underwear" by armed investigators. Frank defended investigators' actions, saying it's "standard protocol" to remove everyone from a house during a raid.

The defense said methods by another investigator, Joseph Warpinski, were flawed and prejudiced against Gallagher from the beginning. Pressed by defense attorney Eric Mukasey, Warpinski acknowledged "there were definitely some mistakes."

Another SEAL deployed to Mosul contradicted allegations Gallagher shot at an elderly man who was a noncombatant during a sniper mission.

Joshua Graffam, who testified under immunity, said he was acting as a spotter for Gallagher -- using binoculars and range finders to help his partner monitor targets -- when he saw two men he thought were ISIS fighters. He told Gallagher, who agreed.

Gallagher fired and appeared to hit one of the men. Graffam said he didn't know what happened to the man, but said he wasn't as old as other witnesses said. He looked to be in his 40s or 50s, he said, and was dressed in all black.

Graffam said Gallagher never took any shots he shouldn't have.

Asked whether he would deploy with Gallagher again, Graffam said he would.

Another witness, Special Operations Master Chief Brian Alazzawi, said no one ever complained about Gallagher shooting at civilians or stabbing a prisoner while on deployment.

Other defense witnesses detailed for the court the trying circumstances Gallagher and the other SEALs were in during their deployment to Mosul.

Andrew Christian, a retired Marine who was deployed to Mosul with Gallagher and his team, said the forces saw combat on a "daily basis." ISIS soldiers were often commanded to fight to the death, he said, and he'd captured ISIS soldiers who dressed as women.

Another Marine, Josh Vanderpool, said Mosul was a "high combat environment" and that Gallagher was sometimes "frustrated" with certain SEALs' work ethics. Gallagher, Vanderpool said, sometimes asked, "What do you guys do to avoid civilian casualties?"

Navy Times has painted a picture of the last moments of the dying ISIS fighter already, using the recollections of SEALs to describe the prisoner struggling to breathe, possibly because of "blast lung," a condition that often affects those who survive explosions like those that rocked his safe house before he was gunned down trying to escape the missile strikes.

Witnesses described a SEAL inserting a chest tube while Gallagher, using a special kit, performed a cricothyroidotomy — or "cric" — a simple and rapid surgical method for opening up a blocked airway by inserting a tube through an incision in the cricothyroid ligament, according to records provided to Navy Times.

But Navy Times also noted that the prisoner's body after 20 minutes of treatment ended up inexplicably spangled with medical devices — a trachea tube, at least two chest tubes and a Sternal Intraosseous Infusion, which bores through bone to reach veins when other IVs won't work, records indicate.

Riffing off the apparent interview of the SO1, the defense motion starts to explain what might have really happened after another SEAL turned off the helmet camera that had been recording the scene.

"At the time that the ISIS fighter was brought to the compound, he was at or near death and, although SOC Gallagher initially attempted to save his life, these efforts quickly proved to be fruitless," the motion stated. "Once it was clear that the ISIS fighter was beyond saving, the platoon's medic ... took over and began using the newly dead or nearly dead ISIS fighter as a training aid to practice performing medical procedures."

7. Andrea Gallagher

Both Andrea and Eddie were originally from Fort Wayne, Indiana. They are approximately the same age. Though they attended different schools, Eddie and Andrea ran in the same circles and met each other when they were around 16 to 17 years old. They became parents when they were young and spent some time apart for a while, possibly when Eddie was deployed, but they reunited in 2006 and married in 2007. She has been a staunch supporter of her husband through all their legal difficulties. The couple are parents to three children: Treven (born 2000), Ava Grace (born 2004), and Ryan Edward Gallagher (born June 2009).

Eddie was arrested on September 11, 2018 at a traumatic brain injury treatment center at Camp Pendleton in San Diego County where he was seeking treatment for injuries incurred during combat duty. Friends said his court-martial trial was particularly hard on the children, but loved ones came to their aid.

Andrea was at the helm of the #FreeEddie campaign and held fundraisers with the help of friends. Eddie's trial began in June and on July 2, a court-martial jury acquitted him of premeditated murder, attempted murder, obstruction of justice, and other offenses. He was found guilty of only one lesser offense—posing for a photo with the young ISIS fighter.

Andrea has been championing her husband's cause ever since he was arrested. She has become a well-known media personality and her work has given her Husband's case national attention.

She started a website, Justice for Eddie, that provides information, news, updates, and raises awareness for Eddie's cause. Andrea also created the "Free Eddie" social media campaign on social media. The Facebook pagefor the campaign currently has over 30K followers.

In addition to social media, Andrea has appeared in several interviews on local and national TV stations such as Fox News to talk about Eddie's case and her campaign to free him.

Her efforts caught the attention of President of Donald Trump who tweeted about Eddie and is considering giving him a full pardo

In honor of his past service to our Country, Navy Seal #EddieGallagher will soon be moved to less restrictive confinement while he awaits his day in court. Process should move quickly

Her website is raising donations for Eddie's cause through the Navy SEALs Fund and she has put on several fundraising events in Florida, San Diego, CA, and Washington DC among others.

https://www.instagram.com/p/BwxcosXHgqE/

Thank you San Diego 🐶 🧧 💯 us We are just amazed at the outpouring of support and love from all of you who attended and made our #FREEEDDIE Fundraiser SUCH A HUGE SUCCESS ♥

She is also posting the same content on her social media accounts for her business "The Better Business Babe". Her Instagram account currently has 37K followers.

The best motherhood advice I could relay: •Motherhood is no joke 🍷▨☐▨ •It's harder to be a good parent than a bad parent. 🧕▨♀☐😊▨ •The days are long but the years are short 😊▨😃▨♀☐👩▨ •My dear friend told me- you only get 18 Summers with your children ❁☐ That one hit me now that I have one in college – adulting ☐▨ • • My babies are growing up but they will always be my babies 💝 So thankful for the honor of being the mother of these amazing humans ☐ • • Happy Mother's Day to all the Mom's out there 😋 • • Proverbs 31:28-30~ 28 Her children arise and call her blessed; her husband also, and he praises her: 29 "Many women do noble things, but you surpass them all." 30 Charm is deceptive, and beauty is fleeting; but a woman who fears the Lord is to be praised. 🙇 ▨

Andrea has three kids with Eddie, 2 sons and 1 daughter. Her oldest son, Treven (18), posted on social media earlier this year to defend his dad and call out the Navy SEALs that turned on him. "You have to understand that SEALs aren't what they used to be, all the badassery really doesn't exist anymore because of shit like this," he said in a series of social media posts. "The new generation of SEALs aren't like those you see who have movies about them.

8. The Verdict

Navy SEAL Eddie Gallagher will have his rank reduced and is sentenced to four months of confinement, which he has already served, for posing with the body of a dead Islamic State fighter, the San Diego jury decided Wednesday.

Gallagher's attorney confirmed that he will retire from the U.S. Navy when he becomes eligible in about three weeks as he hits his 20 years of service.

The SEAL was found not guilty Tuesday on six of the most serious counts he was facing, including premeditated murder, willfully discharging a firearm to endanger human life, retaliation against members of his platoon for reporting his alleged actions, obstruction of justice and the attempted murders of two noncombatants.

"I feel fine. It's all right, you know? The jury came with a verdict. I trust them," Gallagher said after his sentencing Wednesday, which stipulates his rank will be reduced to an E6 paygrade, affecting both his pay and his benefits. A jury also sentenced the SEAL to pay $2,697 per month for four months.

Prior to sentencing, Gallagher's defense succeeded in getting the judge to reduce the potential forfeiture to 50 percent, arguing that some of Gallagher's pre-trial confinement was tantamount to punishment based on the fact that he was denied access to a computer and some medical treatment.

Even though the jury came back with a 4-month partial forfeiture of pay, it will be cut in half, resulting in 2 months partial forfeiture.

He was accused of stabbing to death the 15-year-old combatant in 2017 and posing with the corpse for photos. He endured a dramatic trial where defense attorneys argued that Gallagher's platoon "concocted" the accusations against him, pointing to his history as a decorated SEAL with 19 years of service with multiple tours in Iraq and Afghanistan and earned the Bronze Star with V for Valor twice, a Meritorious Unit Commendation and a trio of Navy and Marine Corps Achievement medals, among other recognitions and decorations.

Nearly a dozen members of Gallagher's platoon testified during the trial against him, revealing that nearly all the platoon members posed for photos with the dead prisoner and witnessed Gallagher read his reenlistment oath near the body, actions prosecutors said proved that Gallagher was "proud" of his actions.

Prior to the sentencing, Lt. Brian John, a Navy prosecutor, warned jurors that "a message needs to be sent" for photos such as the one Gallagher posed for, as they "have [the] potential to fuel propaganda."

"The chief, rather than taking those photos, should have been the one stopping them," he added.

"What is fair?" came the response from Maj. Nelson Candelario, a Marine defense lawyer representing Gallagher during the defense presentation, calling for "no additional punishment."

Gallagher had previously served nine months in prison awaiting trial but was released ahead of trial proceedings at the end of May as the judge attempted to rectify alleged prosecutorial misconduct which included the unauthorized tracking of the defense's emails.

"That's what's fair in this case," he said. "That's what's just."

"It was a regretful decision to pose in the photos," his attorney Tim Parlatore said Wednesday after sentencing. "It obviously was something, if he could take that back he would."

"Chief Gallagher wants that to be a lesson to everybody else, all of the other members of the SEAL community, the Navy, the army the marine corp and all the other services, of your actions have consequences and even though he did not commit a murder, even though he did not do these shootings or anything else, yes he made a mistake with these photos and that's something that every leader, every warrior should think about when they're out there because it can have significant consequences," Parlatore added.

Gallagher, in an interview earlier Wednesday on 'Fox & Friends' alongside his wife, Andrea, and Parlatore, said media reports tried to frame him "as a criminal from the get-go.

"But we knew the truth the whole time," he said. "We knew I was innocent of these charges. I overcame it by having my strong wife with me the whole time and my legal team fighting for me."

The months leading up to his trial were marked with controversy. Defense lawyers and military prosecutors had disputed the conditions of Gallagher's pre-trial treatment, and at one point, even President Trump got involved, tweeting out that Gallagher would be moved to "less restrictive confinement while he awaits his day in court."

Marc Mukasey, one of Gallagher's lawyers who is also President Trump's attorney thanked the president for bringing "this case out of the shadows and into the light."

"America saw what was being done to Eddie Gallagher and thanks to the president for bringing it into the light so that we could expose the injustice that was being done," Mukasey said Wednesday.

Perhaps the biggest bombshell in the case occurred on June 20, when Gallagher's colleague, Special Operator 1st Class Corey Scott, admitted to asphyxiating the ISIS fighter back in 2017, contrary to the testimony of at least seven other SEALs who said Gallagher stabbed the ISIS fighter.

"At that moment, I punched Eddie in the leg and said 'we got him,'" Parlatore recalled.

Gallagher has long held throughout the trial he believes his platoon behaved in a manner not representative of the SEAL community as a whole.

"This has put a black eye on this community. I want the nation to know this is not what our community is about. This community is full of elite warriors that I have been honored and blessed to work with for the past 20 years," Gallagher said.

CPSIA information can be obtained
at www.ICGtesting.com
Printed in the USA
LVHW022038061221
705433LV00017B/3393